LEARNING ABOUT THE EARTH

# Forests

by Emily K. Green

BLASTOFF!
3
READERS

BELLWETHER MEDIA · MINNEAPOLIS, MN

Note to Librarians, Teachers, and Parents:

**Blastoff! Readers** are carefully developed by literacy experts and combine standards-based content with developmentally appropriate text.

**Level 1** provides the most support through repetition of high-frequency words, light text, predictable sentence patterns, and strong visual support.

**Level 2** offers early readers a bit more challenge through varied simple sentences, increased text load, and less repetition of high-frequency words.

**Level 3** advances early-fluent readers toward fluency through increased text and concept load, less reliance on visuals, longer sentences, and more literary language.

Whichever book is right for your reader, Blastoff! Readers are the perfect books to build confidence and encourage a love of reading that will last a lifetime!

This edition first published in 2007 by Bellwether Media.

No part of this publication may be reproduced in whole or in part without written permission of the publisher. For information regarding permission, write to Bellwether Media Inc., Attention: Permissions Department, Post Office Box 1C, Minnetonka, MN 55345-9998.

Library of Congress Cataloging-in-Publication Data
Green, Emily K., 1966-
  Forests / by Emily K. Green.
    p. cm. — (Blastoff! readers) (Learning about the Earth)
Summary: "Simple text and supportive images introduce beginning readers to the physical characteristics and geographic locations of forests."
  Includes bibliographical references and index.
  ISBN 1-60014-036-X (hardcover : alk. paper)
  ISBN-13: 978-1-60014-036-5 (hardcover : alk. paper)
  1. Forests and forestry—Juvenile literature. 2. Physical geography—Juvenile literature. I. Title. II. Series.

SD376.G74 2007
634.9—dc22                                    2006000570

Text copyright © 2007 by Bellwether Media.
Printed in the United States of America.

# Table of Contents

A forest is an area of land covered with trees.

Many different kinds of trees grow in a forest.

**Evergreen** trees grow in some forests. Most evergreen trees have **needles** for their leaves.

The needles do not fall off the trees in autumn. Evergreen forests stay green in winter.

Fir, pine, and spruce
are some kinds of
evergreen trees.

fir ——

pine

spruce ——

**Redwood** trees are evergreens. The redwood forests in California have the tallest trees in the world.

Trees with broad,
flat leaves grow in
some forests.

Most broad, flat leaves change color and fall to the ground in autumn.

Most trees with broad, flat leaves are **bare** in winter. Leaves grow back on the trees in spring and stay green all summer.

Oak, maple, and beech are some kinds of trees with broad, flat leaves.

oak

maple

beech

**Tropical rainforests** grow near the **equator**. These forests always have warm and rainy weather.

Tropical rainforests have more kinds of plants and animals than any other place on Earth.

All forests have trees that stand high above the ground. The tops of the trees make a ceiling called a **canopy**. The canopy shades everything below.

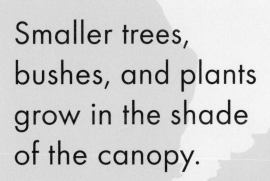

Smaller trees,
bushes, and plants
grow in the shade
of the canopy.

The oldest trees in a forest
die and fall to the ground.

After they fall, the old trees **rot** and turn into dirt. New trees sprout in the dirt. Some day this tree may grow to be the tallest in the forest.

Forests give **shelter** to animals. Birds make their nests in the trees.

Forests take a long time to grow. We need to take care of our forests.

# Glossary

**bare**—trees that have no leaves

**canopy**—a kind of ceiling over the forest made by the overlapping branches of tall trees

**equator**—the imaginary line that goes around the middle of planet Earth

**evergreen**—trees that keep their leaves all through the year

**needles**—sharp spines on some evergreen trees

**redwood**—a very tall evergreen tree

**rainforest**—a kind of forest near the equator where a lot of rain falls all year long

**rot**—to fall apart

**shelter**—a safe place

**tropical**—places that are close to the equator where the weather is warm and rainy

# To Learn More

**AT THE LIBRARY**

Cherry, Lynne. *The Great Kapok Tree: A Tale of the Amazon Rain Forest*. San Diego: Harcourt Brace Jovanovich, 1990.

Gibbons, Gail. *Tell Me, Tree: All About Trees For Kids*. Boston: Little, Brown, and Company, 2002.

de Hugo, Pierre. *In the Forest*. New York: Scholastic, 2001.

Leavell, Chuck. *The Tree Farmer*. Alexandria, VA: VSP Books, 2005.

Pyers, Greg. *Forest Explorer*. Chicago, Ill.: Raintree, 2004.

**ON THE WEB**

Learning more about forests is as easy as 1, 2, 3.

1. Go to www.factsurfer.com

2. Enter "forests" into search box.

3. Click the "Surf" button and you will see a list of related web sites.

With factsurfer.com, finding more information is just a click away.

# Index

The photographs in this book are reproduced through the courtesy of: Frank Krahmer/Getty Images, front cover, p. 19; Stephon Mallon/Getty Images, pp. 4-5; Hirsshi Higuchi/Getty Images, p. 5; Ross M. Horowitz/Getty Images, p. 6; John Burchman/Getty Images, p. 7; Phil Schermeister/Getty Images, pp. 8-9; altrendo nature/Getty Images, p. 8, (top), Ivan, p. 8(middle), Ewa Walicka, p. 8 (bottom); Bryan Brazil, p. 9; Elena Elisseeva, p. 10; Laurance B. Aiuppy/Getty Images, pp.10-11; Theo Allofs/Getty Images, pp. 12-13; Richard Robinson, p. 13 (top), photcay, p. 13 (middle), Kathy Collins, p. 13 (bottom); James Randklev/Getty Images, p. 14; Anup Shah/Getty Images, p. 15; Ulf Sjostedt/Getty Images, pp. 16-17 ; Wes Walker/Getty Images, p. 18; Rich Reid/Getty Images, pp. 20-21.